Henry Parry Liddon

A father in Christ

a sermon preached in St. Paul's Cathedral at the consecration of the Right

Reverend Edward King, D.D.

Henry Parry Liddon

A father in Christ
a sermon preached in St. Paul's Cathedral at the consecration of the Right Reverend Edward King, D.D.

ISBN/EAN: 9783744745147

Printed in Europe, USA, Canada, Australia, Japan

Cover: Foto ©Lupo / pixelio.de

More available books at **www.hansebooks.com**

A Father in Christ

A SERMON PREACHED IN ST. PAUL'S CATHEDRAL,
AT THE CONSECRATION
OF THE RIGHT REVEREND EDWARD KING, D.D.,
LORD BISHOP OF LINCOLN,
AND OF THE RIGHT REVEREND EDWARD HENRY BICKERSTETH, D.D.,
LORD BISHOP OF EXETER,
ON THE FEAST OF ST. MARK THE EVANGELIST, 1885

BY

H. P. LIDDON, D.D., D.C.L.

CANON OF ST. PAUL'S

SECOND EDITION

WITH A NOTICE OF THE REV. DR. HATCH'S PAPER IN THE
"CONTEMPORARY REVIEW," JUNE, 1885

PUBLISHED BY DESIRE

RIVINGTONS

WATERLOO PLACE, LONDON

MDCCCLXXXV

Dr. Hatch has done me the honour of noticing this sermon in the June number of the *Contemporary Review*.[1] His criticism upon it amounts to saying that the Divine origin and obligation of the Episcopate[2] is a "theory," which rests upon a structure of unproved "assumptions;" that it is "only by building assumption upon assumption"[3] that even the precincts of such a "theory" can be reached at all. If I was to carry Dr. Hatch with me, I ought, it seems, to have begun at the very foundation. As it is, I have "assumed," at least at six different points, the truth of positions which he is unable to concede; and the conclusion at which I arrive must therefore, he argues, be regarded as correspondingly precarious and unsubstantial.

Here it may be pleaded that a sermon, from the necessity of the case, must make a certain number of what Dr. Hatch or other persons would call "assumptions," that is to say, statements for which no proof is produced at the time. No preacher, for instance, thinks it necessary to

[1] *Contemporary Review*, June, 1885, art. 8.
[2] *Cont. Rev.*, p. 860. [3] Ib. p. 863.

A 2

repeat in every sermon the arguments which convince him of the existence of God. But a great many educated people in our day unhappily believe that no adequate arguments on this subject are forthcoming; and they consequently regard every reference to God in a sermon as involving an " assumption." A sermon after all is limited by time. And a preacher can rarely hope to do more than handle those considerations which lie nearest to his particular subject, and, perhaps, even only a few of these. Dr. Hatch says with perfect truth that " Dr. Liddon did not attempt to exhaust in a single sermon the arguments by which it " [the Divine origin and obligation of Episcopacy] " has been at various times defended." Certainly, when preaching at St. Paul's, I did not suppose myself to be producing a complete Treatise on Holy Orders. But it was an object with me to touch upon so much of a great subject as might at least show or suggest that a Bishop's consecration was a serious event in the kingdom of Christ; and not an antiquated ceremony which might very well be dispensed with in favour of something simpler, say, a prayer-meeting, conducted by any religiously disposed person who might undertake to conduct it.

I.

Of the six " assumptions " which the sermon is said to make, and which, according to Dr. Hatch, require to be proved, the first, and, incom-

parably the most important, is " the assumption
that Jesus Christ founded, whether mediately or
immediately, a visible society or group of
societies."[4]   Now, in order to prove this " assumption," it is necessary to make another " assumption," which it would take a great deal of time
and space to prove; the assumption, namely,
that the Gospels, and especially the Acts of
the Apostles, are, we will not now say inspired,
but at least trustworthy historical documents,
written by the persons with whose authorship
they are associated, and that they are not com-
pilations or forgeries of a later time, embodying
matter in various degrees legendary and incredible.   Many critics would hold this " assumption "
to be quite as violent and intolerable as any of
those specified by Dr. Hatch.   But unless it may
be made, we cannot discuss the question whether
our Divine Lord did or did not found mediately
or immediately a visible Society or Church.   If,
however, it be allowed, then without going into details which will be familiar to Dr. Hatch, the result
may be expressed in the words of a writer who
is not a clergyman, and who does not appear to
have produced anything in which Dr. Hatch
could detect a " thin streak of sacerdotalism."[5]

"To deny," says Professor Seeley, " that Christ did undertake
to found and to legislate for a new theocratic society, and that
He did claim the office of Judge of mankind, is indeed possible,
but only to those who altogether deny the credibility of the
extant biographies of Christ.   If those biographies be admitted
to be generally trustworthy, then Christ undertook to be what

---

[4] *Cont. Rev.*, p. 861.   [5] *Cont. Rev.*, p. 860.

we have described; if not, then of course this, but also every other account of Him falls to the ground." [6]

Again :—

" It is not more certain that Christ presented Himself to men as the Founder, Legislator, and Judge of a divine society, than it is certain that men have accepted Him in these characters, that the divine society has been founded, that it has lasted nearly two thousand years, that it has extended over a large and the most highly civilized portion of the earth's surface, and that it continues full of vigour at the present day." [7]

And, referring to the Visibility of the Church, the same writer eloquently observes :—

" The city of God, of which the Stoics doubtfully and feebly spoke, was now set up before the eyes of men. It was no insubstantial city, such as we fancy in the clouds, no invisible pattern, such as Plato thought might be laid up in heaven, but a visible corporation, whose members met together to eat bread and drink wine, and into which they were initiated by bodily immersion in water." [8]

And if the question should be raised why the foundation of a Visible Society should enter thus prominently into the work of Our Lord, the reply may best be made in the well-known words of Bishop Butler :—

" Had Moses and the Prophets, Christ and His Apostles, only taught, and by miracles proved, religion to their contemporaries, the benefits of their instructions would have reached but to a small part of mankind. Christianity must have been, in a great degree, sunk and forgot in a very few ages. To prevent this, appears to have been one reason why a Visible Church was instituted: to be, like a city upon a hill, a standing memorial to the world of the duty which we owe our Maker: to call men continually, both by example and instruction, to attend to it,

[6] " Ecce Homo," p. 41.   [7] Ibid. p. 42.
[8] Ibid. p. 136

and by the form of Religion, ever before their eyes, remind them of the reality : to be the repository of the oracles of God : to hold up the light of revelation in aid to that of nature, and propagate it throughout all generations to the end of the world." [9]

But if a Society is to be visible, it must have a certain form and constitution. As Butler again says :—

. . . "This settlement then appearing thus beneficial ; tending in the nature of the thing to answer, and in some degree actually answering, these ends : it is to be remembered, that the very notion of it implies positive institutions ; for the visibility of the Church consists in them. Take away everything of this kind, and you lose the very notion itself. So that if the things now mentioned are advantages, the reason and importance of positive institutions in general is most obvious ; since, without them, these advantages could not be secured to the world. And it is mere idle wantonness, to insist upon knowing the reason. why such particular ones were fixed upon rather than others." [1]

Here Butler seems to anticipate what Dr. Hatch calls my second assumption, namely, that our Lord intended His Church to " have a single form of organization," instead of introducing it to the world in a condition of social chaos. Certainly it is natural to assume this, if we believe Him to be One, of Whose Being order is an eternal law, characterizing His action alike in Nature and in Grace. Indeed Dr. Hatch himself admits that, if there be a visible Society, founded by our Lord, its constitution is a matter of primary importance :—

[9] Bishop Butler, "Analogy," pt. ii. c. 1, p. 151, ed. Oxf. 1844.

[1] Ibid. pp. 151, 152.

"If the Church, of which St. Paul speaks as the Body of Christ, the fulness of Him which filleth all in all, be really, as the Augustinian theory [*rather*, the immemorial doctrine of the Christian Church] assumes it to be, a visible society, or aggregation of societies, then it is a tenable proposition that the Christian ministry is an essential, primary, and authoritative element of the organism of the Christian life, as it came from the Divine Founder." [2]

In point of fact, faith in the visibility of the Church, and in some Divine order of its organization would naturally seem to stand or fall together.

And to this " assumption " it is no objection [3] that our Lord also promises His presence to two or three gathered in His Name: unless the less excludes the greater, and the blessing vouchsafed to a little company of believers, is inconsistent with the foundation and claims of a world-wide and organized Church.

Nor does the " ancillary assumption " of which Dr. Hatch complains, " that the particular form of organization which the Apostles framed or accepted was intended to be permanent," appear to be unwarrantable, if the Holy Spirit was given to the Apostles, as Our Lord promised, to guide His servants into all truth. [4] If "all truth," then, surely, into practical truth when organizing the Church, as well as into speculative truth when preaching the Gospel.   Even " the cardinal doctrines of the existence of sin, and the efficacy of Christ's Redemption," [5] taught by the Apostles, are regarded by many persons as belonging to a state of

---

[2] " Organization of Early Christian Churches," 2nd ed. pref. p. xii.   [3] *Cont. Rev.*, p. 861.
[4] S. John xvi. 13.   [5] *Cont. Rev.*, p. 865.

thought which has had its day; and the Christian
belief in their permanent truth and value is re-
sented as an unproved "assumption."

The earliest Puritans held that the "evangelists" of the Apostolic age were a distinct order
of church officers, and not, as Hooker calls them,
only "presbyters of principal sufficiency whom the
Apostles sent abroad and used as agents in ecclesiastical affairs whenever they saw need."[6] According to Hooker, the Puritan interpretation of
Eph. iv. 11—13 and 1 Cor. xii. 28 proceeds upon
the fallacy of "surmising incompatible offices
where nothing is meant but sundry graces, gifts
and abilities which Christ bestowed."[7] If, therefore, Dr. Hatch asks, why the evangelist was a temporary, while the Bishop is a permanent and necessary feature of Church organization,[8] there is
no necessity of falling back upon a theory of "the
survival of the fittest."[9] It is enough to
reply that the evangelist is only the Bishop himself or one of his clergy when engaged in a
particular field of work, and that the evangelist
never existed excepting in a form in which he may
or does exist at the present day.[1]

---

[6] E. P. V. 78. 7. So, "when the Apostle nameth Pastors
and Teachers what other were they than Presbyters also, how-
beit settled in some certain charge, and thereby differing from
Evangelists?" (ibid.). On the other hand the Prophets were
often, like Agabus, "not to be reckoned with the clergy, because
no man's gifts or qualities can make him a minister of holy
things, unless ordination do give him power," ib. 6.

[7] Ibid. v. 78. 8.   [8] *Cont. Rev.*, p. 862.   [9] Ibid.

[1] The only two persons to whom the word εὐαγγελιστής is

As to the next "two large assumptions," that
" the Apostles had authority to appoint successors
to their own office, and that those successors were
invested with the same powers as the Apostles
themselves," Dr. Hatch credits me with assuming
more than is at all necessary. There are features
of the Apostolic office in respect of which, as is
said in the sermon,[2] the Apostles had no successors. The distinction between these and the
faculties which they transmitted to the Episcopate
has been stated by Bishop Pearson in a passage
which may well be reproduced. He is proving
that " the Episcopal order was instituted in the
persons of the Apostles themselves, and was pro-
pagated by succession from them." " In order,"
he says, " to explain this assertion we must reflect
that a twofold power was granted to the Apostles ;
one extraordinary and for a time, the other ordinary and intended to last. The first-named power
had a twofold reference ; it concerned Christ and
His Church. In respect of Christ, the Apostles
were made especial witnesses of His Resurrection.
In respect of the Church, the House of God, they
were made foundation-stones ; that is to say, they
were appointed and instructed to preach the faith
which had not been before revealed, to found the
Churches, and to gather together the people of

applied in the New Testament are St. Philip and St. Timothy.
Acts xxi. 8 ; 2 Tim. iv. 5. Of these the first was already
a Deacon, the second a Bishop. This may show that in Eph.
iv. 11, the word would not describe an independent office.

[2] Cf. p. 8.

God. The last-named power was that of governing the Churches already founded, of preaching
the word to the body of the faithful, of ministering the sacraments to the people of God, of
ordaining ministers to ecclesiastical offices, of
discharging all things needful for the salvation
of Christians. That which was temporary in the
Apostles was simply and peculiarly Apostolical;
that which was ordinary and enduring was properly Episcopal. They received all power from
Christ. Whatever was personal in them died
with them. Whatever was needed for all ages of
the Church was transmitted during their lifetime
and by their hands to others. Christ said to His
Apostles, ' *As My Father hath sent Me, even so
send I you.*' As He had from the Father a command to teach the people, and to depute ministers
who were needed for this duty and furnished with
the necessary authority, so likewise the Apostles
had the same office and command, with the same
power of choosing ministers, and so on in a con-
tinuous succession to the end of the world. Accordingly, an Apostle is an extraordinary Bishop, and
a Bishop an ordinary Apostle; and thus the Episcopate was founded by Christ in the persons of
the Apostles, and, as existing in the persons of
their successors, it is derived from the Apostles." [3]

[3] Pearson, Minor Theol. Works, vol. i. pp. 283, 284,
Determinatio, Theol. i.:—

"Ordinem episcopalem fuisse in ipsis Apostolis institutum, ac
per successionem ab ipsis propagatum. Ad hanc assertionem
explicandam sciendum est, concessam fuisse Apostolis duplicem

Whether the great author of the Treatise on the Creed, of whom Bentley said that " the very dust of his writings is gold," has been guilty in this passage of making a large and unwarrantable assumption is a point on which it might, I fear, be difficult for me to agree with Dr. Hatch. But it is at least clear that Pearson is not alive to the scruple or embarrassment felt by my critic.[4] Pearson " assumes " that the Apostles had authority to appoint successors to their own

potestatem, temporariam unam et extraordinariam, ordinariam alteram diuque permansuram. Prior potestas duplicem respectum habuit, ad Christum et ad Ecclesiam. Respectu Christi, facti sunt Apostoli peculiares testes resurrectionis Ejus : respectu domus Dei, facti sunt lapides in fundamento ; h.e. ad prædicandam fidem haud prius revelatam, ad fundandas ecclesias, ad colligendum populum Deo, instituti et instructi. Posterior potestas erat regendi ecclesias, jam fundatas, prædicandi verbum fidelibus collectis ; administrandi sacramenta populo Dei, ordinandi ministros ad ecclesiastica munia, peragendi omnia ad salutem Christianorum necessaria. Quod erat in iis temporarium, id erat pure et peculiariter Apostolicum ; quod autem erat ordinarium et perpetuum, idem erat in eisdem proprie episcopale. Acceperunt totam potestatem a Christo : quicquid erat in eis personale, cum ipsis mortuum est ; quicquid erat omnibus Ecclesiæ temporibus necessarium, ipsorum, dum viverent, manibus transmissum est. Dixit Christus Apostolis ' Sicut misit Me Pater, ita et Ego mitto vos." Sicut Ipse habuit a Patre mandatum docendi populum, et ministros ad hoc necessarios, necessariâ auctoritate instructos deputandi ; ita et Apostoli habuerunt idem officium et mandatum, cum eadem potestate ministros eligendi, et ita successive usque ad consummationem sæculi, continuatâ successione. Est itaque Apostolus, episcopus extraordinarius, est episcopus, apostolus ordinarius : atque ita episcopatus fuit in Apostolis a Christo institutus, in successoribus Apostolorum, ab Apostolis derivatus."

[4] *Cont. Rev.*, p. 863.

office, with a limitation in respect of those particulars in which their office was peculiar to
themselves. And if Dr. Hatch considers this
limitation " arbitrary," [5] it must be sufficient to
reply that it arises from the necessity of the
case. The duties of the Apostles were as unique
as were their circumstances. Yet it does not follow
that because the Church could only be founded
once, its founders had nothing to transmit to a
line of successors in the way of spiritual endow-
ments unshared by other people. It is a matter
of fact that St. Paul endowed Titus with his own
power of ordaining presbyters, while yet he
limited Titus' jurisdiction to the Island of Crete.[6]

This reference to Titus involves another assumption which Dr. Hatch has not noticed, but
which is indeed of vital importance to the
discussion. It "assumes" that the Pastoral
Epistles are trustworthy documents; that they
were written, in fact, by the Apostle St. Paul.
In making this " assumption," we must bear in
mind another theory about them, namely, that they
are documents forged at some time in the second
century in order to encounter a formidable and
highly-developed Gnosticism, with the supposed
authority of the Apostle of the Gentiles. According to this theory St. Paul is made to talk a
language, and to be concerned with institutions
which, historically speaking, befit an age later
than his own ; and the forgery—if such it were—
belongs to the same moral, or immoral, category

[5] *Cont. Rev.*, p. 863.   [6] Tit. i. 5.

as do the Pseudo-Isidorian Decretals, which were
designed in the ninth [7] century to reinforce the
growing claims of the Papacy with the pretended
authority of the first Bishops of Rome.   We do
not, of course, assume that Dr. Hatch assents to the
theory of Baur ; but in his Bampton Lectures [8]
he betrays a hesitation on the subject of the
date of the Pastoral Epistles.   In so careful
and well-informed a writer, this hesitation cannot
but occasion anxiety; and he has not dissipated it
in his criticism on my sermon by any distinct
assertion that he believes the epistles to be the
work of St. Paul. [9]

[7] Cf. Decretales Pseudo-Isidorianæ, ed. Hinschius, p. ccxxxv.

[8] "The Organization of the Early Christian Churches," 2nd
ed. p. 83, note.

[9] *Cont. Rev.,* p. 862.   "The office of Evangelist . . . is
mentioned in the Acts, in an Epistle of St. Paul, and in the
Pastoral Epistles."   This of course may be only careless writing.
But it appears to place the Pastoral Epistles in a distinct category from the Epistles of St. Paul.   And it may be right to
point out that the denial of the Pauline authorship of the
Pastoral Epistles involves a very different issue from the denial
of the Pauline authorship of the Epistle to the Hebrews.   The
Epistle to the Hebrews may be believed to have been written in
perfect good faith, even if we should be certain that St. Paul
had nothing whatever to do with it ;—a certainty, however,
which seems to be hardly within the reach of any person who
has carefully considered Biesenthal's *Trostschreiben des Apostel
Paulus an die Hebräer,* p. 19 sqq.   But the Pastoral Epistles
are dishonest documents unless they were written by the Apostle
whose name they bear. They profess to be written by him ; they
employ his authority in order to produce a given effect upon the
belief and practice of the contemporary Church.   It is no adequate answer to say that the ideas of literary honesty current in
the second century must not be measured by those of the nine-

If these Epistles are not what they claim to be, it is impossible to feel much more interest in what an unscrupulous second-century forger, dishonestly using the name of an Apostle for purposes of his own, may have thought or said about an Apostolic Episcopate, than we should feel in the Papal powers ascribed to the primitive Bishops of Rome by the ninth-century fabricator of the Pseudo-Isidorian documents. If, however, in face of a great body of negative criticism, it is still allowable, without "assumption," to consider the Pastoral Epistles as the work of an inspired Apostle, then we may refer Dr. Hatch to Bishop Pearson's well-known vindication against Salmasius of the true teaching of these Epistles, respecting the matter before us.[10] There seems to be nearly as much reason for entertaining Baur's hypothesis, that the Titus and Timothy of the Epistles were very much in the position of archbishops reigning over a number of surrounding suffragans[1] as for supposing

tcenth.   If it could be supposed that the opening words of each of these Epistles—to say nothing of many other statements in them—are intended to create a false impression, it is difficult to see what place they could have in a volume which Christians believe to be a revelation of the Mind of the God of Truth.

[10]   Min. Works, ii. 385 sqq.; Diss. i. de Succ. Prim. Rom. Episc. cap. ix.   Cf. also Hickes' Treatises, iii. 325—328.

[1]   Baur, "Die Sogenannten Pastoralbriefe," p. 85.   Diese ältesten πρεσβύτεροι oder ἐπίσκοποι waren in ihrem Kreise dasselbe, was die spätern Bischöfe waren, und das Verhältniss, in welchem die Apostel zu den πρεσβύτεροι stunden, namentlich Jakobus als Vorsteher der Jerusalemischen Gemeinde zu den πρεσβύτεροι derselben, so wie das Verhältniss des Titus zu den von ihm in Kreta eingesetzten πρεσβύτεροι, des Timotheus

that they had only a temporary commission[2] to do
certain things in Crete and Ephesus, and not a
delegatio perpetua.[3] But even this last-named

zu den πρεσβύτεροι der Ephesinischen Gemeinde, ist nicht so-
wohl dem spätern Verhältniss der Bischöfe zu den Presbytern,
als vielmehr dem Verhältniss der Erzbischöfe zu den Bischöfen
analog. Was daher in den Pastoralbriefen zur Begründung und
Befestigung des kirchlichen Organismus in Hinsicht der
πρεσβύτεροι und ἐπίσκοποι angeordnet und erinnert wird, hat
nichts anders zum Gegenstand, als dieselbe monarchische Ver-
fassung der Kirche, die später vorzugsweise an den Namen der
ἐπίσκοποι geknüpft wird.

[2] This point is admirably discussed by Dean Hickes, ub. sup.

[3] It is observable that in this and other particulars, the
modern opponents of the claims of the Episcopate do little more
than repeat the arguments of those Puritans of the seventeenth
century who proscribed Episcopacy, and made the use of the
Prayer-book a penal offence. See Collier's summary of the
paper of the Parliament Divines against Episcopacy; 'Ecclesiastical History,' viii. p. 342. "They affirm Timothy and Titus
were Evangelists, and seem willing to infer an inconsistency
between this office and an Episcopal character. They pretend
these Saints could not be Bishops because they were not fixed
to a diocese, but frequently removed from place to place. To
the text in the Revelations they answered, Angels of the Churches
was an allegorical addition, and there was no solid arguing from
such figurative expressions." Indeed they seem to have antici-
pated some leading points of my critic's paper in the *Contemporary Review.* Cf. also Collier's account of Dr. Henderson's
two papers, addressed to Charles I. in order to induce him to
sign the solemn league and covenant, and consent to the Bill for
abolishing Episcopacy, ibid. p. 302—305, 306—310. Dr.
Henderson seems to have thought Church government "mutable
and ambulatory:" it would have been difficult for a Puritan
divine, at that moment, to pronounce categorically upon the
rival claims of Presbyterianism and Independency. The associated sects could only agree in a negation; they were at one
in rejecting the immemorial constitution of the Church of
Christ. Dr. Henderson could not, of course, foresee how some

theory would not show that Timothy and Titus
were not properly Bishops, that is, persons who,
besides possessing ministerial power in its fulness,
had also the power of transmitting it. If St.
Paul empowered them to transmit it, the "assumption" that they could do so is not unwarrantable. However, Timothy's position at
Ephesus seems to have been more permanent
than Dr. Hatch supposes. It would appear that
Timothy was commissioned to act as chief pastor
of the Church of Ephesus after St. Paul's decease.
"Watch thou in all things; do the work of an
evangelist; make full proof of thy ministry. For
I am now ready to be offered, and the time of my
departure is at hand." [4] Timothy had the duties
of a missionary or "evangelist" over and above
his position as Bishop of Ephesus. Like
Bishop Smythies at Zanzibar or Bishop Selwyn
in Melanesia, he was an Episcopal Missionary.
If during St. Paul's lifetime he was really a kind
of Vicar-apostolic with episcopal powers, he would
have become after St. Paul's death something
very like a diocesan Bishop. And the theory
which makes Timothy a temporary delegate of St.

of his arguments would one day be pressed against many a book
in the Canon of that Scripture which he quoted, if so mis-
takenly, yet with such an absolute confidence, and,—still more,
—against such central doctrines as those of the Ever-Blessed
Trinity, and the Satisfaction offered by Christ on the Cross,—
doctrines of whose truth he had not a shadow of doubt. But
in theological thought, as in morals, *facilis descensus Averni.*
Only—the "descent" takes time.

[4] 2 Tim. iv. 5, 6.

Paul at least implies that he would have acted fully for St. Paul during the lifetime of that Apostle. If the Apostle says in effect, " Work hard in your office, for I am leaving you," surely he would have left Timothy empowered to transmit what he had received, namely, the faculty of transmitting the ordaining power. If St. Paul meant to provide for a succession of properly-ordained ministers, there would be as much need for the ordaining power after Timothy's death as after his own.

Dr. Hatch says that "the doctrine of the necessity of the Episcopate depends on what must all but be called a curious jugglery of words, upon the hypothesis that the New Testament Bishops are not now Bishops, but presbyters, and that those who are now called Bishops have succeeded to the functions of those who were once called Apostles." [5] What Dr. Hatch represents as a curious jugglery of words, is an instance of the operation of a common law in the history of language. The word " episcopos " is not peculiar in having experienced, both before and after its appearance in the language of Christendom, changes and modifications of meaning. Literature, whether profane or ecclesiastical, is full of words whose meaning has been widened or narrowed, elevated or depressed, with the lapse of time. In the terminology of civil government it is enough to specify such titles as Imperator, Prince, Consul, Duke, Count, Knight, Minister. In ecclesiastical language, Papa or Pope, Archbishop, Dean, Canon,

[5] *Cont. Rev.*, p. 863.

and Hegoumenos, will readily occur to students of
Church history. Dr. Hatch supplies an additional
illustration. He maintains that while such words
as προστασία and προεδρία are used in Eusebius
of the presidency of a Bishop in his Church, they
had been used at an earlier time with reference to
" the whole council of governing officers." [6] Believers in the claims of the highest order of the
Christian ministry are not concerned to deny
that the word by which that order has been
designated since the Sub-apostolic age was applied,
in the age of the Apostles to the order immediately below it; although they may not think that
this admission involves anything that can properly
be described as a " curious jugglery of words." [7]

The " doctrine of the necessity of the Episcopate " is, in fact, independent of any changes of
meaning which may be discoverable in the history
of a particular term. It rests upon the broad
fact that in the Church of the Apostles there was
an order of men, such as were Timothy and Titus,
who notoriously discharged the Apostolic functions
of ordination and chief government in particular
portions of the Church, and who had been
solemnly entrusted with these functions by Apostolic hands. This fact is independent of any

[6] "Organization of Early Christian Churches," 2nd ed. p.
110, note 53.

[7] Leslie, Theol. Works, ii. p. 722, "Qualifications requisite
to Administer the Sacraments," compares the Presbyterian inference from the Apostolic use of πρεσβύτερος and ἐπίσκοπος
with that of persons who would "prove that Christ was but a
Deacon, because He is so called Rom. xv. 8, διάκονος."

question as to the name by which such an order might or might not be known at the time, or as to the names which might at the time be given to the order below it. In that early Apostolic age, language was still uncertain and fluid in some districts of its application; but institutions of Divine or Apostolic origin were already fixed, and their true character is not dependent on variations in the usage of words. The question indeed is not a question of words but of things: and we should have the same problem before us, if the presbyters of our own day were called Bishops on account of their oversight of souls, and our Bishops presbyters, by reason of their dignity and standing.

Dr. Hatch contrasts the uncertainties which, as he thinks, surround the question of the constitution of the Church of Christ, with the "clearness" of the "main facts" of the "Sacred Record."[8] Of course I am as far as possible from implying that the "efficacy of Christ's Redemption" is not "put outside the region of precarious inferences from uncertain phrases," and I rejoice that Dr. Hatch maintains that it is. But he must know as well as any one that a negative criticism, which we can neither ignore nor despise, would hold very different language. And if belief in the Divine Redemption happily survives in popular quarters where belief in the Divine constitution of the Church has perished, this is my reason, not for arguing against what is still accepted from what is denied, but for

[8] *Cont. Rev.*, p. 865.

recommending what is denied as being linked to that which is still, by God's grace, accepted. The difference between the evidence producible for the one set of truths and the other is not so marked as Dr. Hatch appears to imply; and it is to be wished that he would devote the knowledge and power which God has given him to some great effort of Apologetic Theology, so as really to aid that cause of Christian unity which he has at heart.[9]

II.

Dr. Hatch is of opinion that the Ignatian Epistles present a serious difficulty to any one who would maintain that Bishops are successors of the Apostles, and that some suspicion of this difficulty may explain the absence of any reference to them in the sermon.[10] The real reason was that the Ignatian Epistles are a large subject, and a preacher is limited by time. But if the literature of the Sub-apostolic Church were being searched for a vigorous statement of those portions of Christian Truth which the cant phrase of our day brands as Sacerdotalism, it would be natural to turn to the Ignatian Epistles. And when the very references which Dr. Hatch gives in his paper are examined, it is impossible not to be surprised at his courage in suggesting such

[9] " Organization of Early Christian Churches," 2nd ed. pp. 218—222.

[10] *Cont. Rev.*, p. 864.

a writer.   What would some of the more serious
objectors to my sermon say to the following ?

"Let that be considered a valid Eucharist
which takes place under the Bishop, or some
other person to whom he has delegated it."[1]

St. Ignatius insists upon the duty of obedience
to Bishops in terms which he could hardly have
employed, had he been able to hold the opinion
that "the question, whether Episcopacy or Presbyterianism is the more primitive, has merely
an antiquarian interest."[2]   Thus he praises the
Magnesian deacon Zotion, because he obeys the
Bishop, ὡς χάριτι Θεοῦ,[3] and the holy presbyters
as giving way to the Bishop ; "yet not to him, but
to the Bishop of all, the Father of Jesus Christ."[4]

A feigned obedience is not merely a deception
practised on the visible Bishop ; it is an attempt
to deceive the Invisible.[5]   Nominal allegiance to a
Bishop, combined with practical independence of
him, appears to Ignatius inconsistent with keep-
ing a good conscience.[6]   Or take the following
passage from the letter to the Ephesians :—

"Wherefore it is fitting that you concur in the
judgment of your Bishop, as indeed you do.   For
your body of presbyters, worthy of honourable

---

[1] S. Ign. ad Smym. 8.   ἐκείνη βεβαία εὐχαριστία ἡγείσθω, ἡ
ὑπὸ ἐπίσκοπον οὖσα ἢ ᾧ ἂν αὐτὸς ἐπιτρέψῃ.   It may be unnecessary
to add that Dr. Hatch's reasoning on this passage does not seem
to me to be that which it would naturally suggest.—"Organization of Early Christian Churches," 2nd ed. p. 119.

[2] *Cont. Rev.*, p. 861.   [3] Ad Magn. c. 2.
[4] Ibid. 3.   [5] Ibid.
[6] Ibid. 4.   οὐκ εὐσυνείδητοί μοι εἶναι φαίνονται.

mention, worthy of God, is conjoined with their bishop in like fashion as are its chords to a harp." [7]

Again :—

" And while any one sees that the Bishop keeps silence, let him reverence the Bishop all the more; for whosoever be sent by the Father of the Household to take care of His family, it becomes us to receive in such wise as we should Him who sent him." [8]

Passages of this kind, as my critic would know, might be largely multiplied, and they are quoted here, of course, not for his instruction, but for that of readers to whom his manner of referring to Ignatius might happen to convey an inaccurate impression respecting the general tone and teaching of that Saint and Martyr.

Dr. Hatch observes that, " In the view of the writer of these epistles the Bishop stands in the place, not of the Apostles, but of Jesus Christ; the successors of the Apostles are the presbyters." [9] This would seem to imply that if the Bishop represents Jesus Christ, he can have nothing to do with the Apostles; and that if the presbyters succeed the Apostles, they thereby make it impossible for the Bishop to do so too.

Let us examine the passages to which Dr. Hatch refers, as illustrating the mind of St. Ignatius. In the letter to the Magnesians, the Bishop is said to preside in the place of God the Father, while the " most sweet deacons " are en-

---

[7] Ad Eph. 4.   [8] Ibid. 6.   [9] *Cont. Rev.*, p. 864.

trusted with the ministry of Jesus Christ, and the presbyters are in the place of the college of the Apostles.[1]   Here there is no more reason for supposing that the asserted relation of the presbyters to the Apostles excludes an even higher and more direct relation between the Apostles and the Bishop, than for supposing that Ignatius meant to imply that the Bishop and presbyters had no share in the ministry of Jesus Christ, or that the presbyters and deacons in no sense represented the authority of the Father.   Unless we are to call the Bishop (may it be said without irreverence?) a successor of the Father, there is no ground for saying that Ignatius considers the presbyters exclusively to be successors of the Apostles: since the same phrase, εἰς τόπον Θεοῦ—εἰς τόπον συνεδρίου τῶν ἀποστολῶν—is used in both cases.   Ignatius bids the Trallians [2] " do nothing without the Bishop, but to be subject also to the body of presbyters, as to the Apostles of Jesus Christ." Here it may be enough for our purpose to observe that as the higher and more complete sense in which a Bishop succeeds and represents the Apostles does not exclude a certain succession and representation on the part of the presbyters, so, assuredly, it cannot be inferred from Ignatius' reference to this lower relation that he rejects the higher.   Again, St. Ignatius informs the Philadelphians [3] that he himself flies for refuge " to the Gospel as to the flesh of Jesus, and to the

---

[1] Ad. Magn. 6.   [2] Ad Trall. 2.   [3] Ad Phil. 5.

Apostles as to the presbytery of the Church."
That this last expression was suggested by the
ecclesiastical order of presbyters, is improbable:
it is more suggestive of the solemn use of the
word in such passages as Rev. iv. 4, 10; v. 8, 14;
xi. 16; xiv. 3; xix. 4. To the Smyrnæans, St.
Ignatius writes, " All of you follow the Bishop, as
did Jesus Christ the Father, and follow the presbyters as the Apostles, but revere the deacons as
you would a Divine command. Apart from the
Bishop, let no one do anything that affects the
Church." [4]

Then follows the passage already quoted, about
the validity of the Eucharist, when celebrated
under the authority of the Bishop.

Now Dr. Hatch says that " in the view of the
writer of these Epistles the Bishop stands in the
place, not of the Apostles, but of Jesus Christ,
and that the successors of the Apostles are the
presbyters." As a matter of fact, Ignatius in
nine places makes the Bishop represent God the
Father. But what is the exact inference which
Dr. Hatch desires to suggest?

Does he mean that because St. Ignatius makes
the Bishop represent One greater than the
Apostles, therefore he believed him to be something less than what we understand by a successor of the Apostles? Does he mean that, in
the view of Ignatius, Bishops did not succeed the
Apostles at all? Apparently he does mean this
when he writes of the " incompatible view that it

[4] Ad Smyrn. 8.

is presbyters and not Bishops who stand in
the Apostles' places." [5]   Why "incompatible"?
And what is involved in this theory that, according to Ignatius, presbyters were, and Bishops were
not, successors of the Apostles?   Is it meant
that, in the view of Ignatius, a Bishop was in a
higher position than an Apostle, since he represents Jesus Christ? that since Christ is higher
far than the highest Apostle, therefore Christ's
earthly representative must be so too?   And if
this is unimaginable, what is the natural construction of the language of Ignatius?   It is impossible
to read him without seeing that he believed the
Bishop to hold by Divine right the highest visible
authority in the Christian Church.   Such being
his conviction, he must have held implicitly that
the Bishop was a successor of the Apostles; if
only for the reason that, after our Lord's Ascension, the Apostles, while still on earth, had held
the highest visible authority in the Church of
Jesus Christ.   In the Apostolic age itself, every
Christian would have said that the Apostles pre-
eminently represented our Lord among men.   In
the sub-Apostolic age a great Church writer, a
type and leader of the Christians of his day, says
that Bishops do thus pre-eminently represent the
Lord among men.   Is not this to make Bishops,
substantially, successors of the Apostles as well
as something more?

It may be asked why St. Ignatius does constantly speak of presbyters as representing the

[5] *Cont. Rev.*, p. 864.

Apostles ? The answer is that he constantly
thinks of the Apostles not as founding the Church
at, and ruling it after, Pentecost, but as they
were in an earlier time, when working under
our Lord during His earthly life.   This is
why our Lord is, in the view of Ignatius, the
Authority represented by the Bishop, while the
Apostles are represented by the presbyters.   The
earthly head of each Christian Church visibly
represents, according to Ignatius, Christ our Lord,
or, more often, God the Father.   When our Lord
ascended into Heaven, each of His Apostles thus
represented Him ; when the Apostles passed to
their rest,—so Ignatius believed,—each Bishop
represented Him.   If presbyters represented the
Apostles as they were before Pentecost, Bishops
succeeded to all that was not merely personal in
the Apostolic position after Pentecost.   If any one
had asked Ignatius in what light he regarded the
relation of the Bishops of his day to the Apostles,
would he not have answered that the Bishops
had inherited that *status* of the Apostles which
belonged to them as being fully empowered to
represent the Divine Presence within the Church
on earth, and to do for her well-being all that this
representation might imply ? And surely this *is* the
doctrine of the Apostolical-Episcopal Succession.[6]

[6] It would be an injustice to Dr. Hatch to suppose that he
himself attaches any particular value to the authority of St.
Ignatius one way or the other.   Apparently he classes Ignatius
with those " mystics of the early centuries " whose "dreamy
eyes " beheld in their "dark and small " churches " visions
worthy of poets and saints," but which contrast as " a dim world

Another "difficulty" upon which Dr. Hatch lays stress, arises from our Lord's words to St. Peter. If our Lord's words to the Apostles are inherited by the Episcopate, His words to St. Peter, says Dr. Hatch, must be inherited by the Pope. The argument seems to be that either everything said by our Lord to every Apostle must be official, and so somehow transmitted to some successor in the post-Apostolic Church, or else every saying addressed to each and all of the Apostles must be personal, and so must have expired, so far as its scope and operation are concerned, with the Apostles themselves.

Now this dilemma does not seem to be as embarrassing as Dr. Hatch supposes; and it certainly is not adopted by the Church of Rome. Roman Catholics indeed argue, in Dr. Hatch's manner, from the perpetual significance of the words to the Apostles to the perpetual significance of the words to Peter. But St. Peter is not the only Apostle to whom our Lord addressed words of great solemnity in which other Apostles had no share. If He said to one Apostle, " Thou art Peter, and upon this Rock I will build My Church,"[7]

of shadows" with the " present noon " of this nineteenth century. " Organization of the Early Christian Churches," 2nd ed. pp. 111, 112. I therefore understand him to refer to Ignatius merely in the way of an *ad hominem* argument. For a valuable though brief account of the Ignatian writings, and of the support which the testimony to the Divine Constitution of the Church— borne by a man of such different temper, as St. Irenæus—affords to that of Ignatius, cf. Professor Shirley's " Some Account of the Church in its Apostolic Age," pp. 127 sqq. Oxf., 1874.

[7] St. Matt. xvi. 18.

He said to another, " Behold thy Mother." [8]   The
occasion of these last words was more solemn, the
words in themselves surely were not less solemn,
not less ample and suggestive, than was the great
saying to Peter.   If our Lord had addressed to
St. Peter the words which He did address from
His Cross to St. John, what would not Roman
Catholic theologians have made of the unique,
unapproachable relation of the Roman Pontiff to
the Blessed Virgin Mother, and to the Catholic
Church, of which she is unquestionably the fore-
most type ?   As it is, do we ever hear, in any
quarter, from any divine, that the successors of
St. John at Ephesus have any relation, whether
to our Lord's Virgin Mother or to His Church,
which in any way distinguishes them from other
Bishops ?   Plainly here, by universal admission,
was a sublime privilege, involving even a higher
proof of love and confidence than any vouchsafed
to any other Apostle, yet strictly limited to the
Apostle to whom it was vouchsafed, and in no
sense, spiritual or literal, transmitted to his successors.   And the Eastern and English Churches
do but apply to the words to St. Peter the limit-
ing and restricting interpretation which all Catholic
Christendom applies to the precept to St. John.
Undoubtedly a very different interpretation of the
words to Peter has for long prevailed in the
Churches of the Roman obedience.   But the arguments by which this interpretation is shown to be
of comparatively late growth, and of less than

[8] St. John xix. 27.

universal authority, will be as familiar to Dr. Hatch as to myself, and, doubtless, not less convincing.

On the other hand, our Lord's words, "I will give thee the keys of the kingdom of heaven," [9] and "Feed My sheep," [1] addressed to Peter, may be interpreted, as indeed they are commonly interpreted by our divines, not of any unshared prerogatives of Peter, but either of functions belonging to that whole Apostolate which Peter, as *primus inter pares*, unquestionably represented, or else of the ministerial relation of an Apostle to the Church, which Peter had forfeited by his fall, and which he recovered on his repentance. Those who contend that Peter, alone among the Apostles, held "the keys of the kingdom of heaven," ought to go on to maintain that the other Apostles were never made High Stewards of the Household of Christ. Of this Stewardship the key was the badge or symbol; and as soon as its import is thus stated, the question whether the other Apostles had the power of the keys is practically at an end.

Dr. Hatch, indeed, writes :—"If once I accepted Canon Liddon's premisses, the force of an irresistible logic would drive me from the Church of England to the Church of Rome; and not to the Church of Rome only, but to the straitest sect of Ultramontanism." [2]

It would be easy to rejoin by pointing to some positions taken up by my critic, and then show-

[9] St. Matt. xvi. 19.   [1] St. John xxi. 16, 17.
[2] *Cont. Rev.*, p. 864.

ing how, under the guidance of an " irresistible
logic," they might very naturally conduct him or
his readers to conclusions of a much more con-
sistently negative and destructive character than
are any, as I would fain hope, which he at present
accepts. But no doubt, in his case, as in mine,
the impetuosities of fervid logic are sometimes
arrested by the stubborn resistance of intercepting
facts. And it is not for his sake, but for that of
other and younger men, who may be interested in
this discussion, that I would call attention to the
words of a great writer, who reminds us that for
some very serious reasons, an " irresistible logic "
is not always a perfectly trustworthy guide to
theological truth :—

"The region of logic," says the late Professor Mozley, "is a
very plain and very unanimous one, up to a certain line.
Where a thorough agreement and understanding as to any
premisses exist, all competent men will draw the same conclusions from them ; and the inference will command acceptance,
and carry self-evident truth with it. All mankind infer from
the facts before them, that sunshine ripens, that rain makes
things grow, that food nourishes, that fire warms. All men
who knew what a watch was, would infer that it had a maker.
We may go into moral nature—and so far as people understand,
and are agreed upon their moral ground, they will raise the
same inferences upon it—all people, e.g. who appreciate the
fact of a conscience, will infer from it future reward or
punishment. We may come to theology, and so far as men
have a fair agreement and understanding as to any idea, they
will draw the same inference from it. In all these cases the
inferences will be the same, because the premisses, being the
same in people's minds, the inferences are actually contained in
the premisses, and go along with them. But what explains the
commanding irresistibleness of the inferential process at the
same time limits its range. When the inferential process enters

upon a ground where there is not this good understanding, or when it slides out of its own simply inferential functions into conjectural ones and attempts discovery, it loses this command ; and the appeal to simple logic to force unaccepted premisses, or subtle conjectures, will not answer.   On this latter sort of ground, one man's logic will differ from another man's logic ; and one will draw one inference, and another another ; and one will draw more and another less in the same direction of inference.   In this way the logical controversy proceeded on the great doctrines of Christianity in the first centuries : different sects developed them in their own way ; and each sect appealed triumphantly to the logical irresistibleness of its development. The Arian, the Nestorian, the Apollinarian, the Eutychian, the Monothelite developments, each began with a great truth, and each professed to demand one, and only one, treatment for it. All successively had one watchword, and that was, ' Be logical.' Be logical, said the Arian : Jesus Christ is the Son of God ; a son cannot be coeval with his father.   Be logical, said the Nestorian : Jesus Christ was man and was God ; he was therefore two persons.   Be logical, said the Apollinarian : Jesus Christ was not two persons ; he was not, therefore, perfect God and perfect man too.   Be logical, said the Eutychian : Jesus Christ was only one person ; he could therefore only have one nature.   Be logical, said the Monothelite : Jesus Christ was only one person ; He could therefore only have one will.   Be logical, said the Macedonian : the Holy Ghost is the Spirit of the Father, and therefore cannot be a person distinct from the Father.   Be logical, said the Sabellian : God is one, and therefore cannot be three.   Be logical, said the Manichean : evil is not derived from God, and therefore must be an original substance independent of Him.   Be logical, said the Gnostic : an infinite Deity cannot really assume a finite body.   Be logical, said the Novatian : there is only one baptism for the remission of sins ; there is therefore no remission for sin after baptism. Be logical, to come to later times, said the Calvinist : God predestinates, and therefore man has not free will.   Be logical, said the Anabaptist : the Gospel bids us to communicate our goods, and therefore does not sanction property in them.   Be logical, said the Quaker : the Gospel enjoins meekness, and therefore forbids war.   Be logical, says every sect and school :

you admit our premises; you do not admit our conclusions. You are inconsistent. You go a certain way, and then arbitrarily stop. You admit a truth, but do not push it to its legitimate consequences. You are superficial; you want depth. Thus on every kind of question in religion has human logic from the first imposed imperially its own conclusions; and encountered equally imperial counter ones. The truth is, that human reason is liable to error; and to make logic infallible, we must have an infallible logician. Whenever such infallibility speaks to us, if ancient proved tradition be such, or if the contemporary voice of the Universal Church be such, we are bound to obey; but the mere apparent consecutiveness itself, which carries on an idea from one stage to another, is no sort of guarantee, except to the mind of the individual thinker himself. The whole dogmatic creed of the Church has been formed in direct contradiction to such apparent lines of consecutiveness. The Nestorian saw as clearly as his logic could tell him, that two persons must follow from two natures. The Monophysite saw as clearly as his logic could tell him, that one nature must follow from one person. The Arian, the Monothelite, the Manichean, saw as clearly as their logic could tell them on their respective questions, and argued inevitably and convincingly to themselves. To the intellectual imagination of the great heresiarchs of the early ages, the doctrine of our Lord's nature took boldly some one line, and developed continuously and straightforwardly some one idea; it demanded unity and consistency. The Creed of the Church, steering between extremes and uniting opposites, was a timid artificial creation, a work of diplomacy. In a sense they were right. The explanatory Creed of the Church was a diplomatic work; it was diplomatic, because it was faithful. With a shrewdness and nicety like that of some ablest and most sustained course of state-craft and cabinet policy, it went on adhering to a complex original idea, and balancing one tendency in it by another. One heresiarch after another would have infused boldness into it; they appealed to one element and another in it, which they wanted to be developed indefinitely. The Creed kept its middle course, rigidly combining opposites; and a mixed and balanced erection of dogmatic language arose. One can conceive the view which a great heretical mind, like that of Nestorius, e.g., would take of such a course; the keen,

bitter, and almost lofty contempt which—with his logical view
of our Lord inevitably deduced and clearly drawn out in his
own mind—he would cast upon that Creed which obstinately
shrank from the call, and seemed to prefer inconsistency, and to
refuse to carry out truth." [3]

To believe in the Divine origin of the Episco-
pate, and yet not to accept the supremacy of the
Pope, may be, in Dr. Hatch's eyes, "illogical."
But it is the faith of ninety millions of Eastern
Christians. And they hold it, because they
believe, as the best English divines have believed,
that it was also, in the first ages, the faith of
Christendom.

III.

Dr. Hatch's general position is "that the
Christian communities have a free right of
organization, that different forms of organization
have been developed by the force of circumstances
as the ages have gone on, and that the forms of
organization which survive are survivals of the
fittest, and thereby part of the moral government
of God." Such a position would sanction, with
lofty impartiality, all the varieties of ecclesiastical
organization or confusion which have found
shelter from time to time within the widest
boundaries of Christendom. It would sanction,
more emphatically than any other organization,
and as being pre-eminently "a survival," if not "of
the fittest," the Papacy itself; which is obeyed at

[3] "The Theory of Development," by J. B. Mozley, D.D.
Pp. 41—44. London: Rivingtons, 1878.

this moment by the largest number of professing
Christians, and which certainly shows no signs of
approaching dissolution. But it would equally
sanction all those substitutes for the original
and Divine constitution of the Church which the
Church of England kept at bay with so much
deliberation, and after so severe a struggle, in the
sixteenth and seventeenth centuries. It is as
favourable to the wildest Congregationalism as to
the stiffest Presbyterianism, or to the most absolute
Ultramontanism. All forms of Church order are,
according to Dr. Hatch, equally Divine or equally
matters of indifference. But in this absence of
an adequate seriousness, as I must venture to
think it, Dr. Hatch will not enlist the sympathies
of any who believe that the Divine Will, in smaller
matters as in greater, if it can be discovered, is
to be obeyed. For this truly loyal motive under-
lies alike the struggles of the Puritan against
Prelacy, and the struggles of the Ultramontane
against Gallicanism and Anglicanism. And, if the
defenders of particular systems or theories be
mistaken, material error is surely better than indifference to any feature, whether easily discoverable or not, of the Revealed Will of God. When
Dr. Hatch deprecates the "importance which" I
"attach either to organization in itself or to a
particular form of it,"[4] he appears to forget that
in the eyes of believing Churchmen, a Divinely-
ordered organization is not valuable for its own
sake as a piece of mechanism, or as a system of

Cont. Rev., p. 865.

polity, or even as a relic of the past, but because
they hold it to be an integral element of that
Holy Body, through which, by His Spirit, our
Lord quickens and feeds Christian souls.   In
former days Dr. Hatch himself maintained that
the question of Church organization is important,
even if he declined to admit the claims of the
specific organization of the Church.   " It would
appear," he says, with great truth and power, " as
though in the Divine economy which has made
human nature what it is, it is owing, in no small
degree, to the fact of its organization that
Christianity fills the place which it does fill in the
history of the world."⁵   " What it " [Christianity]
" has to do, it does and will do, in and through
organization."⁸   He adds indeed that " the fact of
the necessity and desirability of form is no proof
of the necessity and desirability of this or that
particular form."⁷   But, at least, the admitted
necessity and desirability of some form of organization affords a presumption that the All-
Wise Ruler of His Church would have pointed
with sufficient clearness to one form as in accord-
ance with His Will.   And the Church of England
at least expresses her belief that He has done so
when she makes the authoritative statement that
" it is evident unto all men, diligently reading the
Holy Scripture and ancient authors, that from
the Apostles' time there have been these orders of
ministers in Christ's Church, Bishops, Priests,
and Deacons."⁸

⁵ "Organization of Early Christian Churches," 2nd ed. p. 218.
⁸ Ibid. p. 221.   ⁷ Ibid. p. 218.   ⁸ Preface to the Ordinal.

It is difficult for me to understand how Dr. Hatch reconciles his theory of the unimportance of "a particular form of Church organization," [9] or of the "merely antiquarian" interest of the claims of Episcopacy against Presbyterianism, with the language of the English Prayer-book. Perhaps indeed he may deem any reference to such a subject a "retreat into the fastnesses of dogma." [1] But to say that the service for the Consecration of a Bishop involves at least a serious use of language, s not, I would hope, an excessive "assumption;" and the service appointed in the Prayer-book would appear to take for granted, as its basis and justification, a different estimate of the Episcopal office from that which presents itself to Dr. Hatch. If the Episcopal order is only a surviving relic of antiquity, tolerable and even interesting, but in no real sense necessary to the kingdom and work of Christ, must we not say that the process of admitting a man into it, as prescribed in the Prayer-book, is accompanied by a great deal of needless fuss and verbiage, if not with very irreverent, nay wholly unpardonable appeals to the Most Holy Name? Are we to understand that the most solemn words ever addressed by one minister of Christ to another, might, in the light of a dry criticism, be fairly paraphrased as follows :—" Receive the Holy Ghost for the office and work of a high official in the Church of God, who, however, does not differ in spiritual capacity from anybody else, and who might, indeed, be very

[9] *Cont. Rev.*, p. 865.   [1] Ibid. p. 860.

well dispensed with " ?   Dr. Hatch will be shocked
at this paraphrase of such a sacred form; but is
it not the natural translation of his "theory" of
the Episcopate into modern and practical language?   And are not Christian ministers bound
to consider the practical and religious, as well as
the literary and archæological bearings of an
opinion, before, in a moment of controversial
ecstasy, they expose it to the world in the pages
of a popular Review?

When Dr. Hatch says that "it is incredible,"
that those who do not accept the Church's
teaching respecting the constitution of Christ's
Visible Kingdom, " have no Sacraments, no share
in the communion of saints, and no right to bear
the Christian name," he is uttering a truism.   Or
he is reading his own inferences into a belief
respecting the Episcopate which he avowedly
rejects.   No instructed and believing Churchman
would hold the language which he condemns.
If the non-Episcopal bodies have no true orders,
they have unquestionably a true Baptism, supposing the matter and words of that Sacrament to be
duly administered; since lay baptism is of un-
doubted validity.   And, surely, the great Sacrament of our Regeneration carries with it a share in
the communion of saints, and, much more, a right
to bear the Christian name.   That which, in our
belief and to our sorrow, the non-Episcopal communities lack, is participation in those privileges
which depend upon a ministry duly authorized
by Christ our Lord, and in particular, the pre-

cious Sacrament of His Body and Blood.[2] Even here, when their dissent from His Church is determined by a motive of loyalty to what they believe to be His Will, we may trust that He supplies to them in other ways many blessings which they neglect to seek through the chartered channels. Some men will always say, " I cannot believe that the blessings of the highest communion with Christ are thus conditioned;" just as others will say, " I cannot accept the limitation which is implied in the tremendous words, ' Neither is there salvation in any other ' than Jesus Christ."[4] The human heart must some-

---

[2] Cf. Hughes' Fifth Dissertation pref. to St. Chrys. de Sacerdotio, and qu. in Hickes' Treatises, iii. 407—431.

[3] Acts iv. 12.

[4] Cf. Dean Hickes' Treatises, i. 270. "No strict doctrines are to be rejected for the severity of their consequences upon men who will not believe them, or if they believe them will not practise them, and who perhaps, because they are contrary to their lusts, or their worldly interests and designs, are as contrary to them ; and it may be hate them, and call them ' damning,' ' destroying,' and ' unnatural ' doctrines ; but whatever hard or ugly names our men of large souls may give strict doctrines and principles, they are nevertheless true. By such names libertines may and do call the strict Christian doctrines of sobriety, temperance, chastity, truth, probity, fidelity, patience . . . .; and take upon them to make as it were new Gospels and allowances for themselves, which Christ never made, saying, ' can we suppose,' ' can we believe' that the goodness of God would give us such passions, and so strictly tie us up from the gratification of them ? Can we believe that infinite wisdom and infinite goodness would make us of such a frame, and damn us for doing so and so in such and such circumstances ?" Hickes then proceeds to argue that "as none of those moral doctrines, or those who preach them, can be said to damn the transgressors, but the transgressors, pro-

times make sacrifices at the shrine of faith; but we may be sure that beyond the terms of His Revelation, the Infinite Mercy has resources at His disposal on which we may not presume in our own case, whatever we may hope from them for others. Only when men have real opportunities of knowing God's will, does their opposition to it create anxiety; and indeed while, in perfect good faith, although as we must think, erroneously Presbyterians or Congregationalists stand aloof from the Church or oppose it, they are often

---

perly speaking, damn themselves; so it is not the doctrine of the Divine right of episcopal polity and government, or those who preach it and adhere to it, as necessary by Divine institution, that . . . . ' unchurches the Presbyterian,' and other churches that are not so much as Presbyterian; but . . . . it is they themselves who ' unchurch themselves ' . . . . by wilfully throwing off a government, which was instituted by God for the perpetual, unalterable polity of the Church." (Ibid. p. 271.)

Mr. Gladstone observes that "the genuine Puritans, and the whole Presbyterian body, from Cartwright downwards, contended against the Prelatical constitution of the Church of England," by arguing "that the entire constitution of the Church was defined in the Word of God, and that that constitution was exclusively Presbyterian." "This claim," he says, "was met, not by complaints of its ' unchurching' the Church of England, but by an examination of its matter and foundation." "And sure I am," he proceeds, "that the manly tone of mind and thought which, whatever their faults may have been, distinguished its assertors, would have effectually prevented them, if such a pretension had been as rigorously employed against them, as it was by them, from falling into the feeble-minded and effeminate practice of looking not at its merits, but at the apparent inconvenience of its results."—Gladstone, "Church Principles," pp. 402, 403.

bright examples to many of its professing members.

Like more than one writer in Antiquity, men who live in separation from the Church may teach certain portions of Divine truth with a fulness which is often wanting among ourselves, who have to answer for privileges which they have lost. No Churchman can read Dr. Dale's book on the Atonement or his Commentary on the Ephesians, or Dr. Milligan's work on the Resurrection of our Lord without feelings of warm admiration, and thankfulness to Almighty God for such solid contributions to the cause of true Religion. We should indeed do an ill service to our separated brethren if, in acknowledgment of these or other services to the common Christian cause, we should, in a spirit of facile indifference, compliment away supplemental truths, which as yet they do not accept, and which are not ours to surrender at any man's bidding. But meanwhile their position is at least a consistent one, and they may hope for that increasing illumination which is the reward of consistency. No one can imagine Dr. Dale, with his scholarly perception of the meaning and of the obligations of language, administering or submitting to such a service as the Ordination of Priests in the English Prayer-book, unless he were happily prepared to accept the only belief which redeems it from the imputation of solemn trifling with the Name of God, and with the tenderest sanctities of the human conscience. He may, nay rather he must, think that service to be based on a serious misapprehension of an important side of Christianity; but he knows who and what manner of believers have a moral right to use it intelligently, and who have not.

And if, in past days, we Churchmen have repelled or estranged Dissenters, by our worldliness, by our reliance on an arm of flesh, as shown in our Erastianism, or in exaggerated language respecting our relations with the State, or—worse still—by any ridiculously assumed airs of a fancied social superiority, we have indeed deeply wronged them. Nay, we have wronged that Truth which we hold in trust for them no less than for ourselves. The days have passed when any motive but one should animate a discussion of the questions which divide us. And a unity based, not on indifference or compromise, but on a deeper insight into the value of all the details of God's Revealed Will, and on an increased mutual love and respect, will be more nearly possible when all other aims are indeed governed by the prayer, "That we may grow up unto Him in all things, Which is the Head, even Christ." [5]

H. P. LIDDON.

Christ Church, Oxford, St. Barnabas Day, 1885.

[5] Eph. iv. 15.

" For though ye have ten thousand instructors in Christ, yet have ye not many fathers: for in Christ Jesus I have begotten you through the Gospel."—1 COR. iv. 15.

HERE is a contrast which never disappears altogether from Christendom, but which has not often been more vivid than it was at Corinth in the age of the Apostle. On the one side is a body of active-minded teachers, who within the Christian society are widely listened to and influential; and some of whom, without realizing what Christianity really is and means, evidently aspire on its behalf to meet the cultivated paganism around them on terms of something like intellectual equality. The faith of Christ had not been long enough in Corinth to have entirely forfeited its character of novelty, and they look upon it, possibly from other points of view, but mainly as a valuable stock-in-trade for lectures and dissertations. They are less concerned with its abstract truth than with their own skill in manipulating it. The divisions among the Corinthian Christians are interesting to them, as adding to the general mental fermentation, and as affording numberless opportunities for critical discussion, analysis, perhaps amusement. They are more concerned for their personal reputations than for the moral and spiritual effect upon their hearers of anything that they may say; and their reputations, no doubt, in that small Christian society of Corinth, are, in a sense, brilliant.

On the other side is the Apostle, not less alive to the intellectual aspects of Christianity than are his enterprising opponents, but with a totally different and far loftier conception of its awful meaning. To him it is valuable, not as a stepping-stone to personal importance, but as a message from God to man; as a body of truth compared with which the highest philosophy of this world is foolishness. To his own interests and fame he is sufficiently indifferent; but he is passionately concerned for the well-being of those poor souls at Corinth, and for their practical loyalty to the crucified Redeemer, Who had been the one subject of his preaching among them. He is bowed down with grief and shame at the report of their divisions, which might seem to surrounding heathendom to imply a divided Christ; he thinks cheaply enough of any intellectual activity which was morally so costly. But, if the premises of his opponents were to be granted, no doubt they had the best of it:—"Now ye are full; now ye are rich; ye have reigned as kings without us. . . We are fools for Christ's sake, but ye are wise in Christ; we are weak, but ye are strong; ye are honourable, but we are despised." [1] It is the

---

[1] 1 Cor. iv. 8—10.

contrast between the merely academical and the
pastoral, between a business and a vocation,
between the professor and the Apostle, between
a religion in theory and a religion of practice,
between the intellectual world in its solitary
barrenness and the intellectual world illuminated
and fertilized by the moral, between that which
only interests and occupies the mind and that
which rouses and quickens the conscience, and invi-
gorates the will, and changes and purifies the life.

But there is another point in the comparison
which has yet to be mentioned. The Corinthians
might have—he did not know how many—
lecturers in Christianity at work among them,
sufficiently versatile, clever, witty, even entertaining. Nevertheless only one person could claim
to stand towards them in the sacred and tender
relation of a spiritual father. For to his toil and
prayers alone, under God, did they owe their con
version; and his authority had a claim on them
such as that of no other could possibly rival.
"Though ye have ten thousand instructors in
Christ, yet have ye not many fathers; for, in
Christ Jesus, I have begotten you through the
Gospel."

I.

It would seem that when the Apostle looked
around him for a metaphor which should describe
his relations towards his flock, he could find nothing

in life or nature which so nearly satisfied him as
that of a father.   It is not the only metaphor he
uses to illustrate his Apostolic office.   When
propagating the Gospel he is a husbandman who
plants while another waters ;[2] when struggling
with sin or error he is a soldier in the uniform of
Jesus Christ ;[3] when entreating men to accept
God's promises of mercy in Christ, he is an am-
bassador furnished with Divine credentials ;[4] when
building up the fabric of the Church, or the Divine
Life in souls, he is an architect, greatly concerned
that the foundation of the edifice shall be solid.[5]
But the figure on which his profoundly sympathetic
nature loves to dwell as best expressing his permanent relation to those whom he has won to the
faith of Christ is that which we are considering.

   There is nothing in nature which so resembles
God as a human father ; for the strength, the
majesty, the tenderness, above all, the authority of
the universal Father rests, in a measure, on each
of His earthly representatives.   This was instinctively felt by heathens who, when anxious to
salute a civil ruler by a title that should invest
him with associations such as might take captive
the hearts of his subjects have called him *pater
patriæ*, the father of his country.   This is the
secret of an indefinable dignity that mantles over
the great patriarch whose position is so unique

---

[2] 1 Cor. iii. 6.   [4] 2 Tim. iv. 7.   Cf. 2 Tim. ii. 3.
[4] 2 Cor. v. 20.   [5] 1 Cor. iii. 10, 11.

in the history of the East and in the history of
Revelation; as the father of many nations and the
father of the faithful. The greater clearness and
prominence which the Gospel had given to the
fatherly Attributes of God, had enriched the word
and the idea with a wealth of authority and affec-
tion that men had not before associated with it.
Accordingly, when recommending Timothy to the
respectful sympathy of the Philippians, St. Paul
says that "as a son with the father he hath
served with me in the Gospel." [6] When remind-
ing the Thessalonians of those evangelizing labours
of his which had resulted in their conversion, "Ye
know," he says, "how we exhorted and comforted
and charged every one of you, as a father doth
his children, that ye would walk worthy of God,
Who hath called you unto His kingdom and
glory." [7] Once, indeed, he recognizes in a presbyter this character of spiritual fatherhood.[8]
But, as a rule, he reserves this figure to describe
his own office. "Though ye have ten thousand
instructors in Christ, yet have ye not many
fathers; for in Christ Jesus I have begotten you
through the Gospel."

II.

When we say that Bishops are successors of
the Apostles we are not formulating a theory, but
stating a fact of history. In one sense, indeed,

[6] Phil. ii. 22.   [7] 1 Thess. ii. 11, 12.   [8] 1 Tim. v. 1.

every presbyter succeeds the Apostles; like them,
he ministers the Word and Sacraments of Christ.
In another the Apostles have no successors; they
alone were privileged to found the Church of
Christ, and while founding it to wield a world-
wide jurisdiction. But substantially, and in a
sense all its own, Bishops do, in the phrase of
St. Cyprian, *Apostolis vicariâ ordinatione succe-
dunt.*[9] If they do not singly share in the world-
wide jurisdiction which belonged to the Apostles,
and which could only now be wielded by the
universal Episcopate acting together, they do in
other respects reproduce from age to age among
men the fulness of the Apostolic authority.[1]

There are in the last analysis two, and only
two, coherent theories of the origin and character
of the Christian ministry. Of these one makes
the minister the elected delegate of the congre-
gation; in teaching and ministering he exerts an
authority which he derives from his flock.[2] The

[9] S. Cypr. Ep. 66, ad Florentium, § 4 (ed. Hartel.).

[1] Bramhall, Vindication of the Church of England, Disc. iii.
"Episcopacy was comprehended in the Apostolic office, *tanquam
trigonus in tetragono*, and the distinction was made by the
Apostles, with the approbation of Christ." Works, vol. ii.
p. 69 (Oxf. 1842).

[2] The congregationalist theory appears to confuse election to
a Church office with a commission to discharge it. The first is
from earth, the second from Heaven. Election is the act of the
Christian people: ordination or consecration is the act of Jesus
Christ exerted through the Bishops who represent Him. With
us, it must be owned, an Episcopal Election is now but a
shadow. But the validity of an Episcopal Consecration is in-

other traces ministerial authority to the Person of our Lord Jesus Christ, Who deposited it in its fulness in the College of the Apostles. "All power is given unto Me in heaven and in earth; go ye therefore and make disciples of all nations." [3] "As My Father hath sent Me, even so send I you." [4] The Apostles, thus invested with the plenitude of ministerial power, detached from themselves in the form of distinct grades or orders of ministry, so much as was needed, at successive epochs, for building up and supporting the Church. First, they created an order which was charged with the care of the poor and with the administration of Church funds, although also specially empowered to preach, and to administer the sacrament of baptism. [5] Next they bestowed on the Church a larger separate instalment of ministerial power—that of the presbyters or bishops—as in those first days the second order was called indifferently. [6] To this order full ministerial capacity was committed, excepting the faculty of transmitting the ministry. Lastly, St. Clement of Rome tells us, [7] that desiring

dependent of the machinery which decides who is to be the subject of it.

[3] St. Matt. xxviii. 18, 19.   [4] St. John xx. 31.

[5] Acts vi. 6; vii. 2; viii. 38. 1 Tim. iii. 8—13.

[6] Acts xx. 17, 28. Tit. i. 5, 7. Cf. S. Clem. I. Cor. 42.

[7] S. Clem. I. ad Cor. 44: καὶ οἱ ἀπόστολοι ἡμῶν ἔγνωσαν διὰ τοῦ Κυρίου ἡμῶν ὅτι ἔρις ἔσται ἐπὶ τοῦ ὀνόματος τῆς ἐπισκοπῆς. Διὰ ταύτην οὖν τὴν αἰτίαν πρόγνωσιν εἰληφότες τελείαν

to avoid controversy which they foresaw, the Apostles ordained certain men to the end that when they should have fallen asleep in death others of approved character might succeed to their special office. Such were Timothy and Titus; not yet exclusively called Bishops, but certainly Bishops in the sense of the sub-Apostolic and of our own age; men who in addition to the fulness of ministerial capacity had also the power of transmitting it. In Crete, Titus receives explicit authority from St. Paul to ordain presbyters; at Ephesus, Timothy has particular directions from St. Paul respecting the way in which charges against presbyters are to be received.[8] Thus we see in Timothy and Titus the exercise of what is distinctive both in Episcopal orders and Episcopal jurisdiction; and unless the pastoral epistles are not of Apostolic origin, the three orders existed in their completeness under the eyes of St. Paul. Within the compass of the New Testament there

κατέστησαν τοὺς προειρημένους, καὶ μεταξὺ ἐπινομὴν δεδώκασιν, ὅπως, ἐὰν κοιμηθῶσιν, διαδέξωνται ἕτεροι δεδοκιμασμένοι ἄνδρες τὴν λειτουργίαν αὐτῶν. On the reference of κοιμηθῶσιν see appended note, p. 33. Compare the remarkable statement, quoted by Eusebius (H. E. v. 6) from St. Irenæus, iii. 3. 3 : θεμελιώσαντες οὖν καὶ οἰκοδομήσαντες οἱ μακάριοι ἀπόστολοι τὴν ἐκκλησίαν Λίνῳ τὴν τῆς ἐπισκοπῆς λειτουργίαν ἐνεχείρισαν. Eusebius says (H. E. iii. 2) that Linus became Bishop of Rome after the martyrdom of SS. Peter and Paul. But the language of St. Irenæus, taken alone, might imply that the Apostles made him Bishop of Rome during their lifetime. So Döllinger.

   [8] Tit. i. 5. 1 Tim. v. 19, 20.

are two other facts which point to the establishment of the Episcopate in Apostolic times. One is the position of St. James-the-Less at Jerusalem; he seems to have been an Apostle who already occupied the more localized and restricted position of a Bishop. This appears in the place assigned to him at the Council of Jerusalem,[9] and in the formal visit which St. Paul paid him at a later period,[1] but especially in the unanimous testimony of the second century, which spoke of him as Bishop of Jerusalem.[2] The other fact is the representation in the Apocalypse of the "angels" of the Seven Churches. What were these angels? Guardian spirits of the Churches they cannot have been, since some of them were guilty of grave faults. Nor can they have been the Churches themselves, since St. John distinguishes the angels and the Churches as having the distinct symbols of stars and candlesticks.[3] Each angel represents a Church, for the faith and practice of which he is responsible; and it would be difficult to express more exactly the position of a primitive Bishop.[4]

III.

The origin and claims of the Episcopate is a

---

[9] Acts xv. 13. [1] Acts xxi. 18.
[2] See reff. in Bp. Lightfoot, Philippians, p. 206, note 1.
[3] Rev. i. 20.
[4] Cf. S. Aug. Ep. 43. § 22 : Abp. Trench, Epistles to Seven Churches, pp. 52—57.

district of theology which English divines have
made peculiarly their own.[5] The anti-Episcopal
Puritanism of Elizabeth's reign, represented by
Cartwright, provoked Bishop Bilson's great work
on the "Perpetual Government of Christ's
Church,"[6] and the seventh book of Hooker's
"Ecclesiastical Polity." The more trenchant
Puritanism of the next age necessitated those
deeper studies to which we owe Pearson's
"Vindiciæ,"[7] and Beveridge's annotations on

[5] Perhaps the well-weighed words of Sanderson, as one of
the most illustrious Bishops of Lincoln since the Reformation,
may here be quoted :—"My opinion is that Episcopal Government is not be to derived merely from Apostolical practice or
institution, but that it is originally founded in the Person and
Office of the Messiah, our blessed Lord Jesus Christ, Who, being
sent by His Heavenly Father to be the great Apostle (Heb.
iii. 1), Shepherd, and Bishop (1 Pet. ii. 25) of His Church, and
anointed to that Office immediately after His baptism by John,
with Power and the Holy Ghost (Acts x. 37, 38) descending
then upon Him in a bodily shape (St. Luke iii. 22), did after-
wards before His Ascension into heaven, send and empower His
holy Apostles, giving them the Holy Ghost likewise, as His
Father had given Him, in like manner as His Father had before
sent Him (John xx. 21) to execute the same Apostolical,
Episcopal, and Pastoral Office, for the ordering and governing
of His Church, until His coming again ; and so the same office
to continue in them and their Successors unto the end of the
world (St. Matt. xxviii. 18 – 20)."—Works, vol. v. p. 191, ed.
Jacobson. On the general subject, cf. Bp. Pearson, De Suc-
cessu Prim. Rom. Episc. Diss. i. c. 9 ; Bp. Beveridge, Theol.
Works, vol. i. Serm. i. ii. (Oxf. 1844); Rev. H. J. Rose, On
the Commission and Duties of the Clergy, Serm. ii.

[6] Ed. Eden, Oxf. 1842, pref. vii.

[7] Ed. Churton, Oxf. 1852.

the Apostolical Canons[8]—not to mention the often admirable, but less accurate " Antiquities " of Bingham.

But some English divines may also have felt that when insisting upon the Episcopate as organically necessary to the structure of the visible Body of Christ,—as necessary not merely to its *bene esse*, but to its *esse*,—they were indirectly strengthening a barrier against Ultramontanism.[9] Nothing is more remarkable in this connection than certain debates,[1] both in the second and third meetings of the Council of Trent. The Papal representatives, especially when discussing the question whether a Bishop's residence in his diocese was of divine obligation, or could be dispensed with by the Pope, minimized the authority and rights of the Episcopate down to the very verge of Presbyterianism. Indeed, it may be doubted whether any Presbyterian divine would easily rival the skill of the Jesuit Lainez, when, in a sermon historically famous, he essayed to reduce Episcopal jurisdiction to a shadowy impotence, that would make the way clear for exaggerated assertions of Papal supremacy.[2]

---

[8] Works, vol. xi. xii. ed. Oxf. 1848.

[9] Compare e.g. Skelton, Works, iv. 513, 514, ed. Dubl. 1770.

[1] For the *decision*, see Conc. Trid. sess. xxiii. cap. 4, can. 7.

[2] Philippson, Contre-révolution religieuse au xvie Siècle, pp. 403, 513, 514. So Morinus, De Sac. Eccl. Ord. pars iii. ex. 4, c. 3, 4, gives a list of schoolmen and others who taught " simplicem presbyterum, delegatione Pontificis, posse diaconos et

In our own days the question of Episcopacy is increasingly seen to be bound up with that of the Apostolic origin and authority of the Pastoral Epistles. The critics who, from Schleiermacher down to Baur and Pfleiderer and others, have partly or wholly denied the Apostolic authorship of these Epistles, have insisted with much force and justice upon their so-called hierarchical characteristics;[2] and then they have proceeded to beg a very large question by arguing that these characteristics prove the Epistles to be of post-Apostolic origin. It is also observable that the ablest and the most destructive of recent English speculations on the early organization of the Christian Church omit all reference to these particular books of the New Testament, which, surely, whatever their worth and character, most directly bear on it.

It is, indeed, a solemn question whether we hold the Episcopate to be enjoined by the revealed Will of God, or, like archdeacons and capitular bodies, to be a feature of our Church arrangements, which, however admirable, may conceivably be dispensed with, without sacrificing anything organic in the conditions of communion with

presbyteros ordinare." Even Vasquez, in iii. part. S. Thomæ, diss. 243, art. 3, 4, thinks the opinion probable. Cf. Palmer, On the Church, ii. 410.

[2] See Baur, Die sogenannten Pastoralbriefe, pp. 75—89. Vorlesungen über Neutest. Theologie, p. 344. Pfleiderer, Paulinismus, kap. xi. Holtzmann, Pastoralbriefe, p. 190 *sqq.*

Christ. If, by suppressing Deans and Chapters, we could reconcile all the separated Protestant bodies to the unity and doctrine of the Church, who of us would not gladly make the sacrifice? And if Bishops are not of Divine obligation is it right to uphold a cause and symbol of division with which essential Christianity could dispense? The Protestant historian Ranke[4] has drawn attention to the barrier which is raised by the Episcopate between the English Church and the Lutheran and Reformed communities on the continent. The maintenance of such a barrier is more than intelligible if we believe that upon a true Episcopal succession depends the validity of the Eucharist—our chief means of communion with our Lord. But when we consider the present pressure of infidelity upon all reformed Christendom, is such an obstacle to

[4] Ranke, Hist. Engl. iv. 375. (Oxf. transl.) remarks that at the Restoration, "no one was to obtain an ecclesiastical benefice or be entrusted with a cure of souls who had not been ordained by a bishop." He then endorses the observation that English Churchmen "thus renounced all connection with the Protestant Churches of the Continent." Ib. iii. 495: "Although the Anglican Church rose again, this was balanced by the fact that she had preserved and now restored to its full authority, one of the most important forms of the ancient Church, its Episcopal Constitution." Professor Ranke understands the importance of 1662, as putting an end to any apparent inconsistencies, in respect of the principle of ordination, which may be discoverable in the practice of some members of the Church of England during the preceding century.

unity even defensible, if in our hearts we deem
the Episcopate to be only an archæological
treasure, or only, as the phrase goes, a very
interesting form of Church government ? [5]

IV.

It is time that we should return to the les-
sons which the Apostle would teach us by his
expression " a father in Christ."

The first and great characteristic of the earthly
father is that, under God, he transmits the gift of
physical life.   This is his prerogative distinction;
it most nearly likens him to the Father of heaven ;
it raises his relationship to his children above any
other between human beings.

The Bishop, too, is a father in this sense; that
he alone can transmit ministerial power to others.

[5] By the existing law of the Church of England any Roman
Catholic or Oriental priest may be admitted to a cure of souls,
on producing his Letters of Orders, and subscribing the English
formularies, while the most gifted and experienced of Presbyterian or Congregationalist pastors would have to be ordained
deacon and priest.   This indeed is inevitable if we hold the
Episcopate to be indispensable to the conveyance of a true
ministerial commission.   But if episcopal ordination be only a
matter of ecclesiastical taste, or usage, or propriety, have not our
separated brethren among the Protestant dissenters some right
to complain of the slight which is thus put upon their ministry ?
And if Presbyterian or Congregationalist ministers have been
really ordained, is there no risk of sacrilege in repeating an
ordination?   But cf. Law's Second Letter to Hoadley, p. 31.

" Whereas," says Hooker, " presbyters by such
power as they have received for administration of
the sacraments are able only to beget children
unto God ; Bishops, having power to ordain, do
by virtue thereof create fathers to the people of
God." [6] " The Apostles being Bishops at large,
ordained everywhere presbyters." [7] " Titus and
Timothy having received Episcopal power, as
apostolic ambassadors or legates, the one in Greece
the other in Ephesus, they both did by virtue
thereof likewise ordain, throughout all churches,
deacons and presbyters, within the circuits allotted
unto them." [8]

But was this prerogative shared by presbyters?
The admission of presbyters to lay their hands on
the ordained conjointly with the ordaining Bishop,
as implied in the Pastoral Epistles,[9] and explicitly
recognized by the fourth Council of Carthage,[1]
and in our own Ordinal, does not prove it, any
more than the promise to the Apostles that they
should judge the twelve tribes of Israel confers on
them the office of the one universal Judge.[2] The

---

[6] E. P. vii. 6, 2. [7] Ib. [8] Ib.

[9] 1 Tim. iv. 14 : μετὰ ἐπιθέσεως τῶν χειρῶν τοῦ πρεσβυτερίου.
Cf. 2 Tim. i. 6 : τὸ χάρισμα τοῦ Θεοῦ ὅ ἐστιν ἐν σοὶ διὰ τῆς
ἐπιθέσεως τῶν χειρῶν μου.

[1] Con. Carth. iv. 3 : "Presbyter cum ordinatur, episcopo
eum benedicente, et manum super caput ejus tenente, etiam
omnes presbyteri qui praesentes sunt, manus suas juxta manum
episcopi, super caput illius teneant."

[2] Hooker, ubi sup.

E

presbyters who assist in laying on hands give token of moral approbation and sympathy with the act of the chief pastor; but their presence adds nothing to, as their absence would subtract nothing from, the validity of the rite.

Not that the power of ordination exhausts the creative functions, so to call them, of a Bishop. He is not only a ruler but a parent, not merely a *caput* but a *radix ecclesiæ;* the author or nourisher of all activities for good among those whom he rules. He perpetuates, from age to age, the work of the missionary Bishop in whose chair he sits; and from him every useful effort within the scope of his jurisdiction should receive, if not its original impulse, at least its ready encouragement and consecration. He is by the terms of his office the originating, and creating, and impelling, as well as or rather than the controlling force in his diocese;—it was, perhaps, his keen realization of this aspect of his ministry which made the episcopate of Bishop Wilberforce so fruitful in its results both to his own flock and to the Church at large.

Out of the father's relation to his children, as the earthly author of their life, arises a natural authority which has three distinct departments for its exercise.

The father is the natural teacher of his children. Their intelligence opens under the rays of his instruction. His is the highest wisdom of which they have any experience, and he brings truth home to them by the voice of love. If he cannot himself teach his children, he not only has the right but is under an obligation to choose a substitute; a master who shall stand in his place, and administer that which it is beyond his power to supply.

The Bishop, too, as the father of his diocese, is the one teacher within its limits. In the eye of the Church all the clergy are his substitutes; he can, by the law of the Church, whenever he wills, take their place. This is his *jus magisterii.* Holding as he should in his mind and conscience the deposit of the true faith, his first duty is to see that it is taught to his flock, that it is taught in its integrity, that it is defended when assailed, that it is reasserted in its purity when corrupted or disfigured.[3] For he is not the versatile exponent of a human theory; but the keeper and teacher of a Revelation from God. He can neither reject an old doctrine nor welcome a new one; he can only decide whether a given doctrine which falls in his way is conformable or contrary to the truth which he holds and teaches, and which his spiritual children may expect at his hands. His intellectual outlook will indeed be wide: he will keep his eye as far as may be, on all the surging currents of thought, along which souls are carried hither and thither in our distracted

[3] 1 Tim. i. 3; iii. 2; iv. 13. 16.

modern world; and as he will welcome from any
quarter any ray of truth, so he will pay no feeble
compliments to any shade of error. Before all
things he will be jealous for the honour of our
Lord—His eternal Godhead, His Incarnation in
time, His infallibility as a teacher, the Atoning
power of His Death, the literal truth of His
Resurrection and Ascension and perpetual In-
tercession, the converting and sanctifying in-
fluence of His Spirit, the life-giving and life-
sustaining power which He exerts through His
Sacraments, the endlessness, for weal and woe, of
the life to which He points, beyond the grave.
But an Apostle must trace a Bishop's duties in
this department. " Take heed unto thyself and
unto the doctrine." " Hold fast the form of
sound words which thou hast heard of me, in
faith and love which is in Christ Jesus." " That
good thing which was committed unto thee, keep
by the Holy Ghost which dwelleth in us." " The
things which thou hast heard of me, among many
witnesses, the same commit thou to faithful men
who shall be able to teach others also.[4]

Not only does a father teach; he governs.
Like every society, a family must have a government; and the modern theory of a government
of all by all is not well calculated, at least in a
family, to ensure the general well-being. And
since children lack the requisite experience, and

---

[4] 1 Tim. iv. 16. 2 Tim. i. 13, 14; v. 2.

a mother the necessary vigour, the natural and undisputed ruler is the father.

As the father of his diocese, the Bishop is its ruler. His right to rule is derived, not from a body of electors who have made him, for their common good, a chief magistrate, but from the character which he inherits from the Apostles of Christ. Timothy and Titus are addressed as rulers of Churches; they are to examine the conduct and bearing of their clergy; and in particulars which are specified in detail.[5] They are to see that presbyters who labour in the word and doctrine are counted worthy of double honour.[6] But their rule extends to all descriptions of persons within the Churches over which they have jurisdiction. Timothy is to superintend, according to rules delivered by the Apostle, the ecclesiastical order of widows;[7] Timothy and Titus are to have especial regard to the condition of the numerous Christian slaves;[8] Titus is to look after whole classes of Cretans separately, the young and the old of both sexes.[9]

The Bishop rules, not only the outward circumstances and departments, but also the inner life of his flock; he has, within limits, the *jus liturgicum;* the right and duty of providing that prayers, supplications, intercessions, and eucharists should

[5] 1 Tim iii. 2—13.   Tit. i. 5—9.   [6] 1 Tim. v. 17.
[7] 1 Tim. v. 3—16.   [8] 1 Tim. vi. 1—5.   Tit. iii. 9, 10.
[9] Tit. ii. 2—6.

be made for all men, and especially for all in authority.[1] Everything liturgical, according to primitive Church law, save the matter and form of the Sacraments and the language of the Catholic Creeds, is subject to his discretion. In later ages, as we know, this discretion has been limited almost to the point of annihilation, by Congregations of Rites, and by Acts of Uniformity; yet it may be well, on an occasion like the present, to recall the sense of early Christendom.

But government is impossible in any society without the sanction of punishment. If rules are to be made their violations must be punished; if command is to be a reality, there must be a means of enforcing obedience. The best father who governs but cannot punish would soon discover that the sceptre of his authority was already falling from his feeble hands.

Nor is the Episcopate able to discharge its true duties unless the Bishop can enforce obedience to the faith and discipline of the Church; unless he have some kind of coercive jurisdiction. Already in St. Paul's First Epistle to Timothy, Timothy is addressed as if he were the *judex ordinarius* of a later age. "Against a presbyter receive not an accusation, but before two or three witnesses. Them that sin rebuke before all, that others also may fear. I charge thee before God and the Lord Jesus Christ and the elect angels, that thou

[1] 1 Tim. ii. 1, 2.

observe these things without preferring one before another, doing nothing by partiality."[2] In the same sense Hymenæus and Alexander are pointed out to Timothy as having "made shipwreck concerning the faith," and as having been " delivered unto Satan."[3] And to Titus the order runs: "A man that is an heretic, after the first and second admonition, reject."[4]

V.

The fatherly character of the Bishop is sometimes traversed by the accidents of age or attainments. He may find among his clergy men who are older, or more generally accomplished, or better divines, or of higher spiritual experience than himself. Of these the best will always echo St. Jerome's exclamation to St. Augustine— " Amice carissime, ætate fili, dignitate parens."[5] They will remember that a Bishop's fatherly character is independent of his personal characteristics; that it belongs to an office which comes from Christ.

A like result may follow on the relations of the Church to the civil law. We may well, indeed, be grateful to the law for the position which it secures to the clergy by making every benefice a

---

[2] 1 Tim. v. 19—21.   [3] 1 Tim. i. 20.   [4] Tit. iii. 10.
[5] Ep. 71. ad. Aug. Opp. iv. pars ii. p. 613 (ed. Martianay).

freehold; yet a freehold may be converted into a fortified castle, from within whose walls a rebellious son sets at nought the counsels of a spiritual father. But that which of late years has most frequently veiled from the eyes of his clergy the kindly face and hand of a father in Christ is the unhappy fact that under the form of interpreting documents which have a legal aspect, the most sacred questions of doctrine and morals are not decided in the last resort by the commissioned guardians of the faith, but by accomplished lawyers, who may or may not be Christians. This fatal weakness in our Church polity was aggravated by the provisions of the Public Worship Regulation Act. We can indeed defend existing arrangements if we can suppose that St. Paul would have allowed the questions pending between himself and the Galatian Judaizers, or the Corinthian deniers of the Resurrection, to be settled by the nearest proconsul. Only those who wish ill to the English Church can desire to perpetuate a state of things which is not necessary to the union of Church and State, or to the maintenance of the Queen's Supremacy, and which, among the many mischiefs which it entails, does more than anything else to impair, in the eyes of faithful clergy, the fatherly character of the Episcopate.

But a father does not, unless in the last extremity, insist upon his rights; he takes them for granted;

he recommends them to his children by the
love which makes authority more than welcome.
When the machinery of Church government,
especially in its penal aspects, is rudely exposed
to view, it is plain that there has been somewhere
a serious failure in duty.

So delicate a relationship as that of a father in
God does not depend for its working efficacy on
the amount of authority which can be arrogated for
one side, or on the submission which can be ex-
torted from the other. It depends on moral in-
fluences; on the respect which is inspired by high
and disinterested character; on the attraction
which is exerted by a true love of God and man.
Like the most beautiful things in the moral world,
this authority is of tender growth, and it is easily
impaired or forfeited. A scornful or impatient
word, scarcely intended by the irritated and,
perhaps, over-worked speaker, will rankle for
years in the mind of a young curate, and colour
his whole conception of the relation in which he
stands to the fathers of the Church.

It is difficult to say how much is lost to the
moral force of the Church and to the character of
her ministers when a Bishop is thought and
spoken of as a good man of business, or a man
who might have been a judge, or a very accurate
scholar, or even a well-read divine, if besides and
beyond all these he is not recognized as the father
of his flock, both lay and clerical; the one man

to whom men instinctively turn for advice and
counsel in moments of moral or mental perplexity ;
the man on whose wide knowledge and kindly
temper and simple disinterestedness of purpose
they know that they can depend for trustworthy
guidance ; and of whom they think habitually as
of one whose blessing would be dearly prized as
a message of encouragement from another world
in the dark hours when its shadows are already
falling thick across the path of life.

VI.

Of public institutions in modern Europe the
Episcopate is in years the most venerable. It is
older than any secular throne ; it is by some centuries older than the Papacy, which was an out-
growth from circumstances unknown to the first
Bishops of Rome.[6] The Episcopate had reached its
prime while the Empire was still standing. It could
shed its blood with Cyprian ; it could illuminate

---

[6] Professor Hussey observes that the first step towards the
establishment of the supremacy of the See of Rome was taken
"in the fourth century," when an appellate jurisdiction was
given to its Bishop by the Council of Sardica, A.D. 347. "Then
for the first time the precedence among equals, willingly con-
ceded to Rome in early ages, was turned into a claim of
authority." Rise of the Papal Power, by Robert Hussey, B.D.,
late Reg. Prof. of Eccl. Hist., Oxford, Clarendon Press, 1863.
2nd. Ed. Lect. i. p. 1, note 3, and especially Pref. p. xxxii.

the world by the consecrated genius of an Irenæus, of an Augustine, of Chrysostom and Basil and the Gregories. It seemed to undergo a weird transformation at the hands of feudalism. We think of the Bishops clad in mail armour who fought at Senlac or in the wars of Stephen, or of later prelates whose brasses in our older cathedrals represent them as blessing us in cope and mitre out of their battlemented castles. Of the sixteen sculptured compartments which record the events of the episcopate of Guido Torlati at Arezzo, only the first, in which he takes possession of his see, and the last, when he lies upon his deathbed, exhibit him in any pastoral charater or have any relation to his work as a father in Christ. After the soldier Bishops come the great statesmen; it requires an effort to recollect the true character of Wolsey and Richelieu, or of certain of those prince-electors who so largely swayed the fortunes of Germany. Then appeared the literary Bishops; men often greater in profane than in sacred letters. And now, as in many other ways so in this, we are apparently re-entering upon the earliest conditions of the Church's life. But the intervening periods were not, as we may too hastily think, periods during which the real objects of the Episcopate were utterly lost sight of. The soldiers, the diplomatists, the men of general literature were always a small minority of their order, which as a whole, quietly and unostenta-

tiously pursued its course of ruling churches and
guiding souls.   Let us remind ourselves of such
language as that of the Sixth Council of Arles,
held at a time when the Bishops of France were
largely great feudatories under Charlemagne.
" Let the Bishops bear in mind," says the 17th
Canon, " that they are intrusted with the care of
the people and of the poor, as their guardians
and protectors.   If, then, they see the unfortunate
oppressed by the powerful and the highly placed,
let them charitably remonstrate; and, if their
advice is disregarded, let them carry their complaints to the Sovereign, that he may correct by
his supreme authority those who would pay no
regard to the advice of their pastor."   And as
for Wolsey, let us not recall the years when—
the most powerful statesman in Europe—he was
wont to appear in this cathedral as Legate *a latere,*
and indeed, proudly held the balance between
France and the Empire; let us think of the
discredited and broken man who had retired from
the Court of the sensual Tudor to his northern
diocese, there to win almost at once the hearts of
the clergy and the poor by his pastoral care
and tenderness.[8]   The Episcopate as it traverses
the centuries is like a weather-beaten barque on
whose hull clusters many a shell and weed that

[7] Conc. Arelat. vi. (a. 813) can. 17. Hefele, Concilien-
geschichte, iii. p. 757.
[8] Cavendish, Life of Wolsey, p. 202 (ed. Morley).

tells of the seas of feudal or political life behind it; but as these encrustations fall away we discover that the essential features of a spiritual fatherhood, which were always there, remain intact. The title, father in God, has never disappeared from the language whether of the Church, or of the law, or of general literature ; and the reality, even in the worst times, has never been without a witness. The century which beheld Hoadley on the English bench was also the century in which men knelt down in the streets of London to ask for the blessing of Bishop Wilson.

VII.

Certainly we meet to-day on an occasion when we may insist on this characteristic of the highest order in the sacred ministry with more than usual hope and confidence. The eminent scholar and poet, not less saintly in his life than remarkable for his acquirements, who has lately left us, is to be succeeded in the see of St. Hugh by one whose nomination has thrilled the hearts of his brother Churchmen with the deepest thankfulness and joy. Never, probably, in our time has the great grace of sympathy, controlled and directed by a clear sense of the nature and sacredness of revealed truth, achieved so much among so many young men as has been achieved, first at the Theological College of Cuddesdon, and then from the Pastoral Chair at Oxford, in the case of my dear and honoured friend. He is surrounded at this solemn moment by hundreds who know and feel that to his care and patience, to his skill and courage, to his faith and spiritual insight, they owe all that is most precious in life, and most certain to uphold them in the hour of death; and their sympathies and prayers are shared by many others who are absent from us in body, but present with us in spirit. Certainly, if past experience is any guarantee of what is to come, if there be such a thing as continuity of spiritual character and purpose, then we may hope to witness an episcopate, which κατὰ τὰς προαγούσας προφητείας [9]—if current anticipations are not wholly at fault—will rank hereafter with those which in point of moral beauty stand highest on the roll of the later English Church—with Andrewes, with Kenn, with Wilson, with Hamilton.

And, if I may not presume to speak from such personal knowledge of the successor of our own Bishop in the great see of the West, it is at least allowable to dwell on the hopes which gather round an honoured name, and on the wide reputation for devotion and spiritual experience which has been gained by a long and fruitful ministry in this metropolis. He, too, will carry with him into his new field of labour the prayers and sympathies of grateful friends, known and unknown, who

[9] 1 Tim. i. 18.

earnestly desire that he may long rule and feed
his flock in the fulness of the blessing of the
gospel of Christ.

Men say that hard times are coming upon the
English Church; and, outside her walls, voices,
like those of the children of Edom in the day of
Jerusalem, may even now be heard to cry,
"Down with her; down with her; even to the
ground." And, in truth, she has already lost
much which was of no mean value for our
Master's service. The Education Act of 1870 has
largely withdrawn the people from her schools;
and recent legislation has swept away all but a
rapidly diminishing fragment of her old position
at the Universities. With largely secularized
populations, with our higher class increasingly
trained by infidel teachers, and with our vastly
extended franchise, it is not unnatural to anticipate for the Church in the coming years sterner
experiences than have befallen her since the middle
of the seventeenth century. But the prospect is
by no means an entirely dark one; and among its
brighter features is the wealth of generous devotion
which young men and women in increasing num-
bers, and of various conditions in society, are
freely offering almost day by day to the sacred
cause of our Lord and Saviour. It is as though
the anxieties of a loved and aged parent could
open and melt hearts which were closed against
her in days of more assured prosperity; and surely

no token of God's present favour could inspire more courage for dealing with the problems that may be in store for her sons. To all who are thus, in their opening life, giving their best to God, the event of this day will be full of encouragement and of hope. For it is the consecration to the highest duties in the Church of sympathies which, next to His own supernatural grace, have drawn them, most persuasively, to the feet of the Redeemer; it is an assurance that they will find on Apostolic thrones that union of tenderness and wisdom which recalls while it transcends all that is most revered and loved in an earthly home.

APPENDIX.

On the quotation from St. Clement 1 Cor. 44, at p. 9, note 6.

To whom do κοιμηθῶσιν and αὐτῶν refer in this passage ? Bp. Lightfoot (in loc. and Phil. 201 sqq.), and, less decidedly, Prof. Funk (in loc.) answer, To the προειρημένοι, i.e. " the first generation of presbyters appointed by the Apostles themselves." On the other hand, Rothe (Anfänge der Christl. Kirche, p. 378, sqq.) and Brüll (Tubingen Theol. Quartalschrift, 1876, p. 445, sqq., qu. by Funk) refer the words to the Apostles.

1. In support of this latter opinion it may first of all be observed that ἐάν is used before κοιμηθῶσιν. If St. Clement meant to say that the Apostles appointed A.B.C. as presbyters, and provided that when A.B.C. died, D.E.F. should succeed them as presbyters, why did he say " *if* they should fall asleep " ? Why not " when " ? Of course, in time A.B.C. *would* die, and other ministers would be needed to succeed them. Whereas if κοιμηθῶσιν be referred to the Apostles, ἐάν glances at the contingency of the Apostles dying before the presbyters whom they had ordained ; —a contingency in view of which they made provision that others should succeed to their own power of ordaining presbyters.

2. Next, in the clause immediately following that quoted at p. 9, the words occur, τοὺς οὖν κατασταθέντας ὑπ᾽ἐκείνων ἢ μεταξὺ ὑφ᾽ ἑτέρων ἐλλογίμων ἀνδρῶν . . . . . τούτους οὐ δικαίως νομίζομεν ἀποβάλλεσθαι τῆς λειτουργίας. Now the ἕτεροι ἐλλόγιμοι ἄνδρες here mentioned show what kind of persons are meant by the δεδοκιμασμένοι ἄνδρες immediately above. To make the two phrases denote different classes of persons would involve the context in hopeless confusion. Who, then, are the ἕτεροι ἐλλόγιμοι ἄνδρες ? They are persons who after the death of the Apostles, appoint or ordain ministers as the Apostles had done. The point

F

of the sentence is that as the function of ordination belonged
originally to the Apostles, so it belonged subsequently to the
ἐλλόγιμοι ἄνδρες : and thus that if a man was ordained by
an ἐλλόγιμος ἀνήρ he had as good a ministerial *status* as if he
had been ordained by St. Peter or St. Paul. The practical
inference for the Corinthians was that to disturb that
status would be as grave an offence in the one case as in
the other. So understood, the second sentence throws light
upon the first: it leads us to see in the first a provision
made by the Apostles for supplying the Church with future
ordainers, in the persons of certain δεδοκιμασμένοι ἄνδρες, who
were to act in that capacity, in the event of the death of the
Apostles. This construction of the first sentence is far from
being foreign to St. Clement's purpose. For the Corinthian
ministers in behalf of whose rights St. Clement is protesting
had been apparently ordained by some ἐλλόγιμοι or δεδοκιμασμένοι
ἄνδρες, i.e. sub-apostolic men of the rank of Timothy and Titus ;
and to establish the commission of these ordainers was to vindi-
cate the rights of those whom they had ordained. It will be seen
that on this construction of the passage there are no persons but
the Apostles to whom κοιμηθῶσιν and αὐτῶν could refer. And,
indeed, if St. Clement had meant to refer κοιμηθῶσιν to the
προειρημένοι, while δεδώκασιν (Funk ἔδωκαν) is said of the
Apostles, he must surely have indicated the change of subject
by writing ἐὰν οὗτοι κοιμηθῶσιν.

The substance of this note is largely indebted to my kind
friend, Professor Bright. Cf. Beginnings of the Christian
Church, by Rev. W. H. Simcox, p. 214. Theological Critic, ed.
T. K. Arnold, vol. i. p. 242. Bp. Pearson sees in the passage
St. Clement's account of the way in which " ipse ad Episco-
patum promotus est." Diss. ii. de annis prim. Rom. Episc.
4. 3. Min. Wks. ii. 456. The general sense of the language
is well summed up by Haddan, Apost. Succ. p. 106, although
he refers κοιμηθῶσιν to οἱ προειρημένοι, and by Mr. Gladstone,
Church Principles, p. 215. The discussion in Langen's
Geschichte der Römischen Kirche, p. 80, is interesting, although apparently open to objections, some of which have been
already stated or implied.